W9-BSM-964

SMART ABOUT SPORTS

Soccer in Western Europe

By

Mike Kennedy

with Mark Stewart

NORWOODHOUSE PRESS

Norwood House Press, P.O. Box 316598, Chicago, Illinois 60631

For information regarding Norwood House Press,
please visit our website at: www.norwoodhousepress.com or call 866-565-2900.

Photo Credits:
  All interior photos provided by Getty Images.
Cover Photos:
  Top Left: Topps Trading Cards.
  Top Right: Javier Soriano/AFP/Getty Images.
  Bottom Left: Andreas Rentz/Getty Images.
  Bottom Right: The Upper Deck Company.
The soccer memorabilia photographed for this book is part of the authors' collections:
  Page 10) Robben: Topps Trading Cards.
  Page 12) Beckenbauer: Fax Pax; Cruyff: Match! Magazine; Platini: Trebor Barratt Ltd.;
          Schmeichel: The Upper Deck. Company.
  Page 13) Van Basten: The Upper Deck Company; Baggio: The Upper Deck Company;
          Bompastor: The Upper Deck Company; Ronaldo: The Upper Deck Company.

Designer: Ron Jaffe
Project Management: Black Book Partners, LLC
Editorial Production: Jessica McCulloch
Special thanks to Ben and Bill Gould

Library of Congress Cataloging-in-Publication Data
  Kennedy, Mike, 1965-
    Soccer in Western Europe / by Mike Kennedy, with Mark Stewart.
      p. cm. -- (Smart about sports)
    Includes bibliographical references and index.
    Summary: "An introductory look at soccer teams and their fans in western
  Europe including France, Italy, Greece, and Spain. Includes a brief history,
  facts, photos, records, and glossary"--Provided by publisher.
    ISBN-13: 978-1-59953-447-3 (library edition : alk. paper)
    ISBN-10: 1-59953-447-9 (library edition : alk. paper)
    1. Soccer--Europe, Western--Juvenile literature. 2. Soccer teams--Europe,
  Western--Juvenile literature. I. Stewart, Mark, 1960- II. Title.
    GV944.E85K46 2011
    796.334094--dc22

                        2010046568

Manufactured in the United States of America in North Mankato, Minnesota.
170N–012011

Contents

Words in **bold type** are defined on page 24.

Spain is a world power in soccer.

Where in the World?

In Western Europe, soccer is part of everyday life. Children start kicking a ball as soon as they can walk. Everyone always wants to know, "Did my team win today?"

Once Upon a Time

Soccer came to Western Europe in the 1800s. Workers and students brought the game with them from England. Soon there were great teams in Italy, Austria, Germany, and France.

The Italian team celebrates in 1934.

Two teams begin a match in Allianz Arena.

At the Stadium

Allianz Arena in Germany is always busy. It is home to three teams. Some people think that Allianz Arena looks like a space ship from the outside.

Town & Country

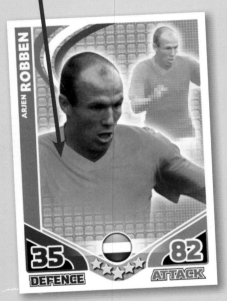

Arjen Robben of the Netherlands plays for two teams. All the best players in Western Europe do the same. In 2010, Robben played for a **club** in Germany. When his home country of the Netherlands had a match, he joined the **national team**.

Arjen Robben
plays for his
German team.

Shoe Box

The sports collection on these pages belongs to the authors. It shows some o the top Western European soccer stars.

Franz Beckenbauer

Defender • Germany
Franz Beckenbauer was a great player and a great leader.

WORLD CUP WONDERS

No. 21   Johan Cruyff (Holland)

Johan Cruyff

Midfielder • Netherlands
Johan Cruyff roamed all over the field to score goals.

Michel Platini

Midfielder • France
Michel Platini was one of Western Europe's best players ever.

Peter Schmeichel

Goalkeeper • Denmark
Peter Schmeichel used his big body to stop goals.

World Cup USA 94

Peter Schmeichel

Marco Van Basten

Striker • Netherlands
Marco Van Basten used power and grace to become a great scorer.

Roberto Baggio

Striker • Italy
Roberto Baggio scored in the **World Cup** in 1990, 1994, and 1998.

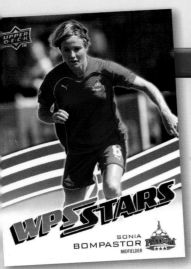

Sonia Bompastor

Midfielder • France
Sonia Bompastor was good at scoring goals and stopping them, too.

Cristiano Ronaldo

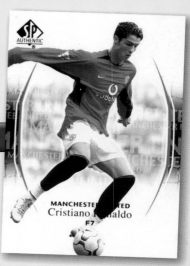

Forward • Portugal
Cristiano Ronaldo became a star as a teenager.

Can't
Touch This

The only players allowed to touch the ball with their hands are the goalkeepers. They must be quick, smart, and brave. When a shot is moving toward the net, goalkeepers must be ready for anything!

Nadine Angerer of Germany catches a ball in midair.

Oh no! Arne Friedrich of Germany is given a yellow card.

Just For Kicks

Watching soccer is more fun when you know some of the rules:

- When a player makes a dangerous or unfair play, the referee calls a foul.

- The punishment for tripping, pushing, and holding is a **free kick**.

- For a very dangerous foul, a player is warned with a yellow card.

- A red card means a player is out of the game.

On the Map

Girls and boys play soccer all over Western Europe, including these countries:

1. Austria
2. Belgium
3. Denmark
4. Finland
5. France
6. Germany
7. Greece
8. Italy
9. Netherlands
10. Norway
11. Portugal
12. Spain
13. Sweden
14. Switzerland

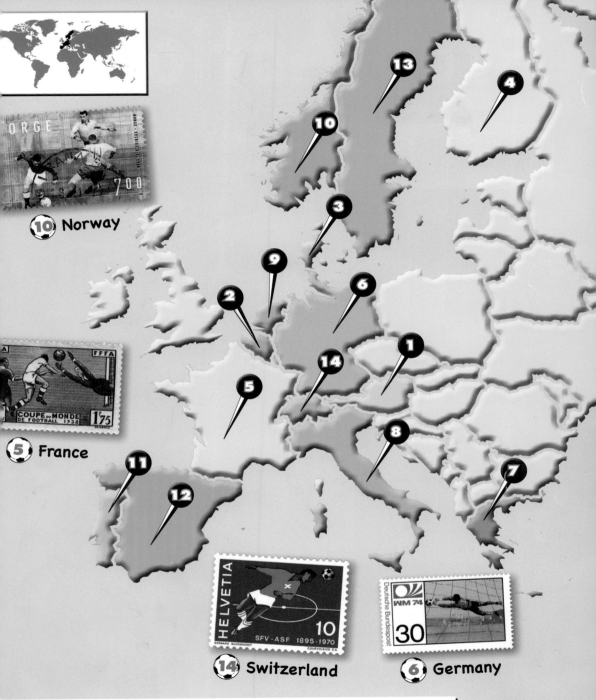

10 Norway

5 France

14 Switzerland

6 Germany

Many countries have their own soccer stamps!

Stop Action

Sergio Ramos of Spain plays defense.

Dirk Kuyt wears the orange uniform of the Netherlands.

Pedro Rodriguez of Spain watches the ball.

All players wear long socks.

21

We Won!

Western Europe has some of the best teams in the world!

Men's Soccer	World Cup Champion
Italy	1934, 1938, 1982, & 2006
West Germany*	1954, 1974, & 1990
France	1998
Spain	2010

Women's Soccer	World Cup Champion
Norway	1995
Germany	2003 & 2007

* West Germany is now part of Germany.

Birgit Prinz leads the cheers for Germany in 2007.

Soccer Words

CLUB
Another word for team.

FREE KICK
A shot given to a team after a foul has been called.

NATIONAL TEAM
A team made up of players from the same country.

WORLD CUP
The tournament that decides the world champion of soccer. The World Cup is played every four years.

Index

Photos are on **bold** numbered pages.

Learn More

Learn more about the World Cup at www.fifa.com

Learn more about men's soccer at www.mlssoccer.com

Learn more about women's soccer at www.womensprosoccer.com